I AM NOT AN EGGBOX

THE RECYCLING PROJECT BOOK

Published in 2020 by Welbeck Children's
An imprint of Welbeck Children's Limited, part of Welbeck Publishing Group.
20 Mortimer Street London W1T 3JW

Text & design © Welbeck Children's Limited, part of Welbeck Publishing Group

First published in 2018 by Carlton Books Limited

A CIP catalogue record for this book is available from the British Library

ISBN: 978-1-78312-416-9

Printed in Dongguan, China
10 9 8 7 6 5 4

Author: Sara Stanford
Creative Director: Clare Baggaley
Written, designed, illustrated and packaged by: Dynamo Limited
Design Manager: Emily Clarke
Senior Production Controller: Yael Steinitz
Executive Editor: Stephanie Stahl
Publisher: Russell McLean

The publishers would like to thank the following sources for their kind
permission to reproduce the pictures in this book.
Shutterstock: /Imageman: 41 (lentils); /Dmitrii Kazitsyn: 41 (pasta);
/Olga Popova: 41 (beans); /M. Unal Ozmen: 41 (corn & rice).

I AM NOT AN EGGBOX

THE RECYCLING PROJECT BOOK

WELBECK

AMAZING THINGS TO MAKE WITH EGGBOXES!

Hi THERE!

DO YOU WANT TO KNOW HOW TO TURN YOUR UNWANTED EGGBOXES INTO ARTY MASTERPIECES?

LOOK NO FURTHER, BECAUSE INSIDE THIS BRILLIANT BOOK YOU'LL BE MAKING EVERYTHING FROM PENGUINS TO PIRATE SHIPS AND ALL THINGS IN BETWEEN! TURN THE PAGE FOR CRAFTY CREATIONS GALORE. LET'S GO!

YOU'LL NEED A GROWN-UP TO HELP YOU WITH ALL OF THE MAKES!

YOU WILL NEED

- 10 EGGBOXES IN VARIOUS SIZES
- COLOURFUL PAPER
- COLOURFUL CARD
- TISSUE PAPER
- GLUE
- TAPE
- SAFETY SCISSORS

- TIN FOIL
- PAINTS
- PAINT BRUSHES
- RULER
- STRAWS
- BOTTLE TOPS
- BUTTONS
- FEATHERS

- LOLLYPOP STICKS
- PIPE CLEANERS
- STRING
- GOOGLY EYES

CONTENTS

PENGUIN!

I'M YOUR **POCKET** SIZED **PENGUIN** PAL AND I'M **READY** TO PLAY.

LET'S GO FISHING.

MADE FROM AN EGGBOX - ME?
NO WAY!

YOU WILL NEED

- ONE EGGBOX
- SAFETY SCISSORS
- TAPE
- WHITE AND BLACK PAINT
- PAINT BRUSHES
- ORANGE PAPER OR CARD
- GLUE
- GOOGLY EYES

SET THE SCENE

You can make a whole waddle of penguins as well as a chilly ice-scape for them to play on. Scrunch up some tissue paper, then flatten it out a bit and stick it to a piece of card to make a snowy background. Follow the step-by-step guide on the next page to make your frosty friends.

DID YOU KNOW?

A GROUP OF PENGUINS ON LAND IS CALLED A 'WADDLE'.

EGGBOXES CAN'T **WADDLE** THROUGH SNOW WITH ORANGE **FLIPPERS**, OR GO FISHING IN iCY **WATERS**.

GO FURTHER!

MAKE THESE MINI MONSTERS USING THE SAME TECHNIQUE. TURN OVER TO FIND OUT HOW!

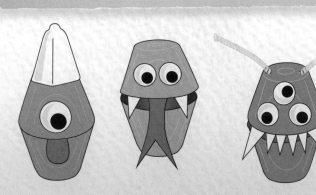

I AM NOT AN EGGBOX...
I'M A PENGUIN!

1

To make the body of your penguin pal, carefully cut two egg cups out of an eggbox.

2

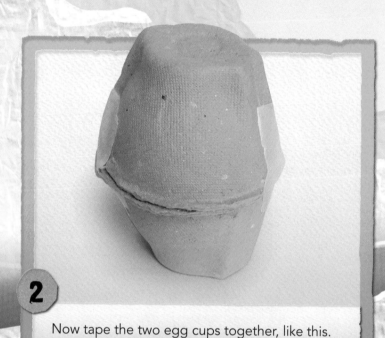

Now tape the two egg cups together, like this.

3

Paint a white oval to make a tummy for your penguin and then leave it to dry.

4

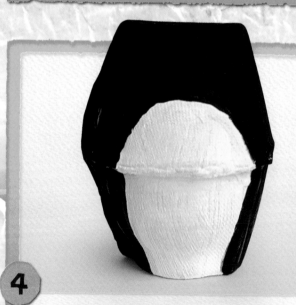

Next, paint the rest of your penguin black. Leave this to dry while you go on to Step 5.

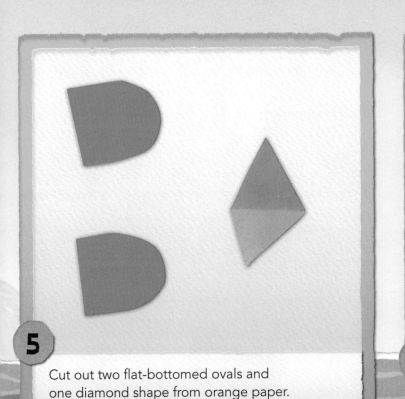

5

Cut out two flat-bottomed ovals and one diamond shape from orange paper. Fold the diamond in half to make a beak.

6

Glue the beak and flippers onto your penguin and add some googly eyes from your book!

I AM NOT AN EGGBOX...

I'M A MINI MONSTER!

Tape two eggbox cups together in the same way as Steps 1 and 2. Paint all over in brightly-coloured monster shades, then get creative with your monster faces. Cut fangs and tongues out of coloured paper and make horns out of pipe cleaners. Finish off with some googly eyes.

OWL!

I PERCH **UP HIGH** IN **A TREE**. I SLEEP **UP HERE** IN THE DAY AND I FLY ABOUT **ALL NIGHT**.

COULD AN **EGGBOX** EVER BE AS **WISE** AS ME?

YOU WILL NEED

- ONE EGGBOX
- SAFETY SCISSORS
- PAINTS
- PAINT BRUSHES
- FEATHERS
- GLUE
- BROWN PAPER
- GLUE

SET THE SCENE

Draw a large tree trunk on a sheet of paper. Place your eggbox owls on the branches to make them feel right at home. You could then cover the branches with real leaves. Turn the page to see how to give an eggbox its own set of feathers.

FANCY MAKING A BIRD MASK? GO TO THE NEXT PAGE.

I'M AN OWL!

1

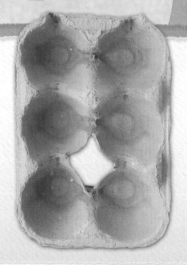

First take off the lid of the eggbox, leaving you with the base. Carefully cut out one of the spaces in the middle, to look like this.

2

Paint your eggbox brown, leaving out the two top cups and the space between.

3

When the brown paint is dry, paint the cups white to make eyes, and the space between yellow to make a beak. Now leave to dry.

4

Next, glue on some colourful feathers to cover the middle of the owl. You can choose any feathers you like.

5

Cut two triangles out of the leftover eggbox lid and paint them brown. Then tape them in place at the top of your owl for ears.

6

Add two blobs of black paint for the owl's eyes, or use your googly eyes!

I AM NOT AN EGGBOX...

I'M A BIRD MASK!

Snip out the top section of an eggbox, like this, to create your eye mask. Decorate it with sequins, buttons, and colourful feathers. Carefully make a hole on each side of the mask and thread string or ribbon through to tie it behind your head, or tape one side to a paper straw.

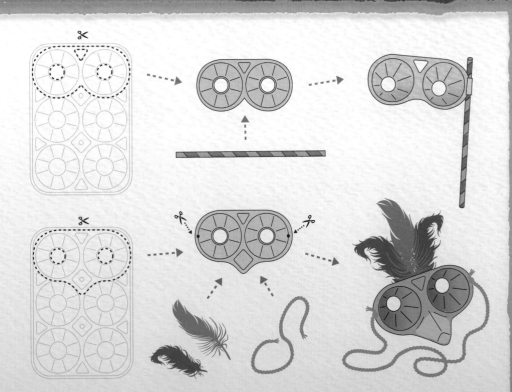

13

FIRE ENGINE!

NEE-NAW! WHEN THE FIRE ALARM RINGS, I WILL BE THERE IN A FLASH TO **SAVE THE DAY** AND **KEEP** THE CITY **SAFE**.

EGGBOXES CAN'T BE **HEROES**, SO THAT'S WHY I **MUST** BE A REAL FIRE ENGINE!

VROOM!

YOU WILL NEED

- ONE LARGE EGGBOX
- SAFETY SCISSORS
- RED PAINT
- PAINT BRUSHES
- BLUE PAPER
- GLUE
- TWO STRAWS
- CARD
- TAPE
- ONE PIPE CLEANER
- BOTTLE TOPS OR BUTTONS
- TIN FOIL
- YELLOW PAPER

SET THE SCENE

Create your own city background for your fire engine. Cut lots of different-sized rectangles from coloured paper, then line them up across a large sheet of white paper to make your skyline. Now it's time to put your engine to the test. Turn over to start making!

DID YOU KNOW?

THE 'JAWS OF LIFE' IS A TOOL ON A FIRE ENGINE THAT RESCUES PEOPLE STUCK IN BUILDINGS OR CARS.

GO FURTHER!

ON THE NEXT PAGE YOU'LL SEE HOW TO MAKE A TERRIFIC TRUCK, AS WELL AS YOUR FIRE ENGINE!

TO THE RESCUE!

I AM NOT AN EGGBOX...
I'M A FIRE ENGINE!

1 Carefully cut away part of the eggbox lid, like this. Then, paint it red all over and leave it to dry.

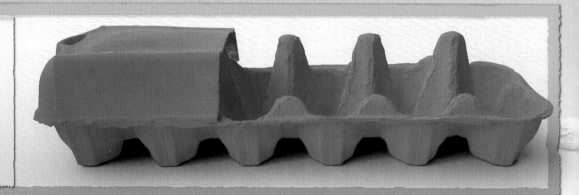

2 Cut two squares and three rectangles out of blue paper to make windows and a windscreen, then glue them in place.

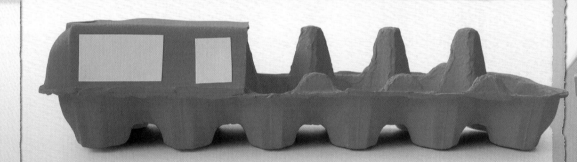

3 Join two straws together by taping small strips of card from one straw to the other. Keep taping more strips of card in the same way until you have a complete ladder.

4 Now, roll a pipe cleaner into a coil to make a firefighter's hose.

5

Add lights by gluing colourful buttons to the top of your engine. Use two small balls of tin foil for headlights and glue more buttons to the sides to make the wheels.

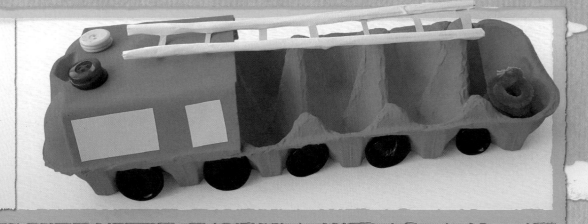

6

Paint red stripes onto thin strips of yellow paper to decorate your engine. Hooray! You're ready for your first rescue mission.

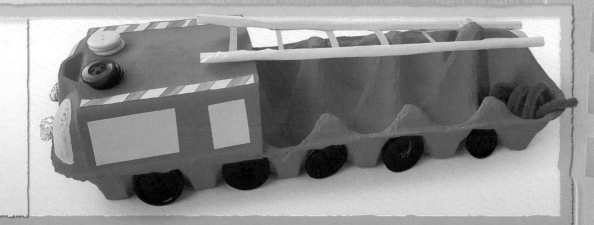

I AM NOT AN EGGBOX...
I'M A TRUCK!

To make your truck, cut a smaller eggbox in the same way as the fire engine. Paint it any colour you like. You can still add your windows and button wheels, but you don't need to make a ladder or a hose this time. Easy!

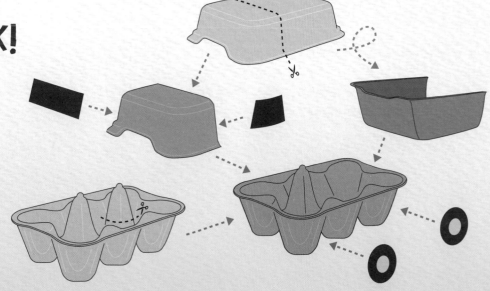

HEN!

CLUCK, CLUCK, CLUCK,

YOU'LL FIND ME WITH MY FABULOUS FEATHERS STRUTTING ABOUT ON THE FARM AND PECKING AT SEEDS.

YOU WILL NEED

- ONE EGGBOX
- RED AND WHITE PAINTS
- BRUSHES
- SAFETY SCISSORS
- WHITE CARD
- GLUE OR TAPE
- PENS
- GOOGLY EYES

SET THE SCENE

Make a fantastic farm for your hen by tearing green paper to make rolling hills. Use brown paper or paint to add a barn. Find out how to make a hen buddy to hold all your secret storage goodies when you turn the page.

18

GO FURTHER!

FEEL EVEN MORE SPRING-LIKE WITH THESE BEAUTIFUL DAFFODILS! TURN THE PAGE TO FIND OUT HOW TO MAKE THEM.

I SUPPOSE I DO HAVE ONE THING IN COMMON WITH AN EGGBOX...

...BUT i AM WAY MORE FABULOUS!

I AM NOT AN EGGBOX...

I'M A HEN!

1

Paint your eggbox white all over and then leave it to dry while you do Step 2.

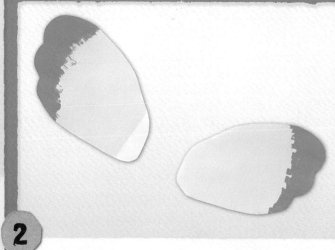

2

Cut out two wing shapes from white card and paint the tips red, like this. Leave them to dry.

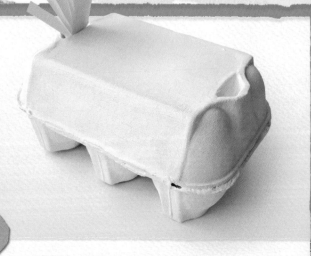

3

For the tail, cut out five to ten strips of white card (each one around 5cm long) and tape them to the end of your eggbox in a fan.

4

When your wings are dry, tape or glue them to either side of the eggbox.

5 Draw your hen's head and neck on white card and carefully it cut it out. Paint on your hen's face and beak, then stick on some googly eyes and leave to dry.

6 Finally, fold over the end of your hen's neck to make a tab to tape onto your eggbox.

I AM NOT AN EGGBOX...

I'M A BUNCH OF DAFFODILS

Cut the cups out of your eggbox, then trim the edges to make a flower shape as shown. Paint them yellow and add an orange button to the centre. Glue each one onto a green straw and cut leaves out of green paper. Tie together to finish your bouquet!

CRAB!

COME AND PLAY WITH ME AT THE **BEACH** AND **SCUTTLE** ALONG THE **SAND**!

WATCH OUT! I HAVE **TWO** GREAT **BIG PINCERS** AND PLENTY OF **LEGS**.

I DON'T **CARRY SHELLS** I'VE **GOT MY OWN...**

YOU WILL NEED

- ONE EGGBOX
- SAFETY SCISSORS
- ORANGE PAINT
- ORANGE PIPE CLEANERS
- TAPE
- GOOGLY EYES
- PEN

SET THE SCENE

Make a crafty rock pool for your eggbox crabs by scrunching up brown paper bags. Place them around a pool made from a blue piece of paper or card. Turn over for a step-by-step guide on how to make your friend.

Turn over for a step-by-step guide on how to make your friend.

DID YOU KNOW?
CRABS HAVE TEN LEGS AND THIS MAKES THEM DECAPODS.

PINCH!

PINCH!

GO FURTHER!

LOVE CREEPY CRAWLIES? YOU CAN LEARN HOW TO MAKE THESE LITTLE BUGS ON THE NEXT PAGE.

ON THE NEXT PAGE.

I'M A CRAB!

1

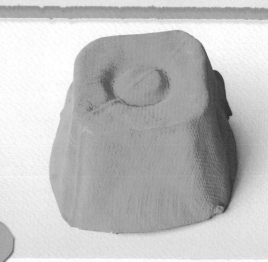

Cut one cup out of your eggbox and paint it bright orange. Leave it to one side to dry.

2

For each pincer, cut one orange pipe cleaner 10cm long and bend it in half. Wrap a small piece of pipe cleaner to each end, like this.

3

Now tape the pipe cleaners underneath the egg cup so the pincers are at the front of the body.

4

Cut eight strips of pipe cleaner about 6cm long each. Now fold each strip into a curved leg shape.

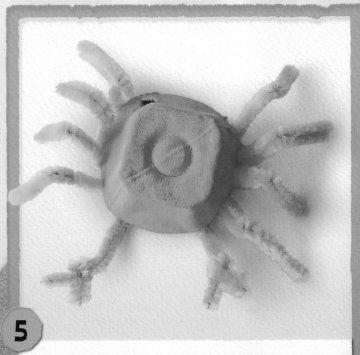

5

Tape all your legs underneath the egg cup. Make sure there are four on each side.

6

Stick on some googly eyes from your book and draw a big smile to finish.

I AM NOT AN EGGBOX...
I AM A BUG!

Make lots of different creepy crawlies using the same technique! To make a caterpillar, cut out a row of cups from your eggbox, paint them and thread them together with a pipe cleaner. You could stick the googly eyes onto antenna made from pipe cleaners as well. Paint your cups black to make a spider, or red with black spots to make a ladybird.

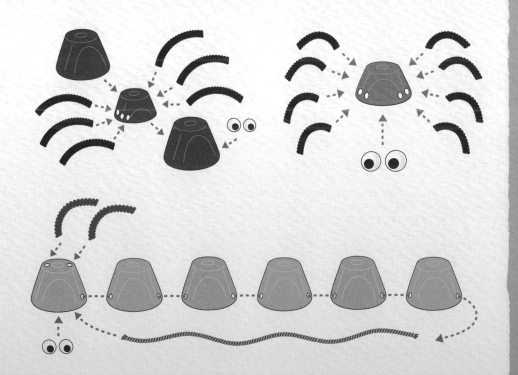

PIRATE SHIP!

I SAIL THE **SEVEN SEAS** WITH A DECK FULL OF **PIRATES**, STOPPING OFF AT **DESERT ISLANDS** IN SEARCH OF BURIED **TREASURE**.

AAARRRRRR!

YOU WILL NEED

- ONE LARGE EGGBOX (FOR 12 EGGS)
- YELLOW AND BROWN PAINT
- SAFETY SCISSORS
- RED PAPER
- LOLLIPOP STICKS
- TAPE
- BLACK CARD
- STRING OR COTTON
- COLOURFUL PAPER
- BLACK OR WHITE PAPER

DID YOU KNOW?
PIRATES WERE SUPERSTITIOUS AND THOUGHT THAT WHISTLING ON A SHIP WOULD BRING ON STORMS.

SET THE SCENE

Tear strips of yellow, orange and white paper (you can use old magazines if you like!) and glue them to a piece of blue paper to make a collage island in the middle of the seven seas. Now turn over the page to make your pirate ship.

STORMY WEATHER WON'T GET IN THE WAY OF ME AND MY QUEST FOR TREASURE, OH NO!

GO FURTHER!

MAKE A WHOLE FLEET OF MINI BATTLESHIPS USING EGG CARTON CUPS. TURN OVER TO FIND OUT HOW!

I'M A PIRATE SHIP!

1

Carefully cut the lid away from your eggbox, then paint the outside brown and the inside yellow. Leave this to one side to dry.

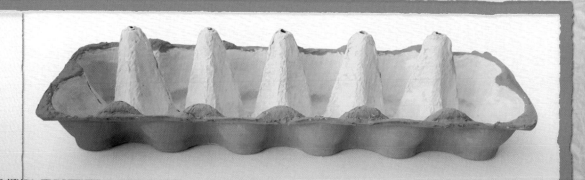

2

To make a sail, cut out a paper rectangle (around 15cm by 12cm). Snip a slit into the top and bottom of the flag to thread the lollipop stick through. Make two sails and tape them to your ship.

3

Cut out an anchor shape from black card and tape a length of string or cotton to the top. Tape the other end to your ship.

4

Make bunting by cutting small triangles from colourful paper. Fold each triangle over some string or cotton and tape in place.

5

Give your ship an extra pirate touch by making a Jolly Roger flag. Ahoy, me hearties!

I AM NOT AN EGGBOX...

I AM A BATTLESHIP!

To make a fleet of mini ships, cut out the cups from your eggbox and paint them brown. Wrap rectangles of white paper around toothpicks to make the sails, and a diamond of black paper to make a pirate flag (don't forget the skull and crossbones!). Add a ball of plasticine to your boat and stick in your toothpick sails.

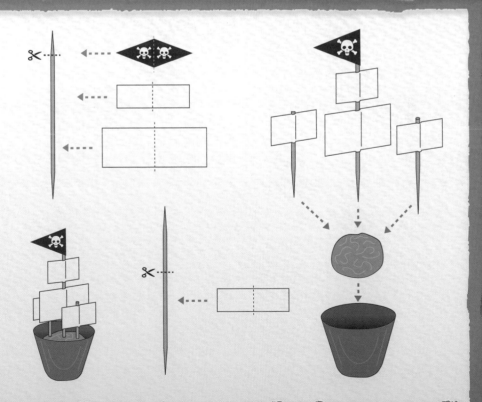

DRAGON!

I AM A **FIRE-BREATHING DRAGON**, NOT JUST SOME OLD EGGBOX.

I LOVE TO **SOAR** HIGH UP IN THE **CLOUDS** AND **ALL OVER** THE LAND.

ROAR!

SET THE SCENE

Make a fairytale setting full of forests and mountains by sticking different shades of green paper on top of each other and painting on trees. On the next page you can make your own dragon to soar over the landscape. What are you waiting for?

YOU WILL NEED

- ONE BIG EGGBOX (FOR 12 EGGS)
- GREEN PAINT
- BLACK PEN OR PAINT
- TWO BOTTLE TOPS
- WHITE PAPER
- SAFETY SCISSORS
- GLUE AND TAPE
- YELLOW AND WHITE PAPER
- TISSUE PAPER
- TAPE

WITH MY **FANGS** AND **SPIKES**, IT CAN BE HARD TO MAKE **FRIENDS**!

ROAR!

GO FURTHER!

DON'T STOP THERE... YOU CAN MAKE
A SLITHERING SNAKE WITH A FORKED
TONGUE ON THE NEXT PAGE.

I'M A DRAGON!

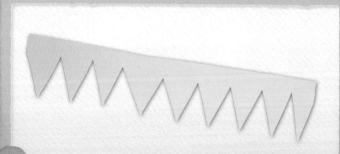

1 Paint your eggbox green all over and leave it to dry. Then paint or draw on some black nostrils.

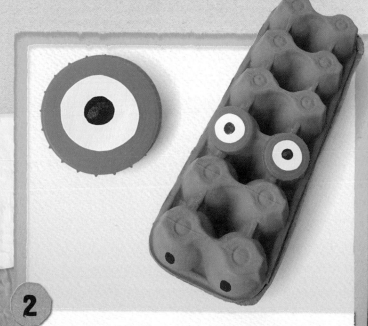

2 For the eyes, cut out two white circles and stick them onto green bottle tops. Paint or draw some black pupils, then stick these onto your dragon.

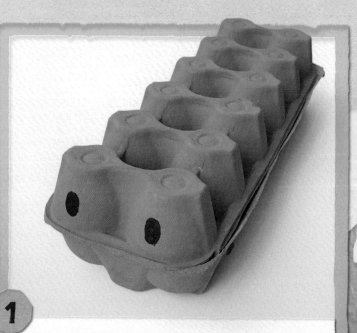

3 Next, cut a strip of zigzags out of a piece of yellow paper. It should be long enough to reach down the dragon's back. Tape it in place.

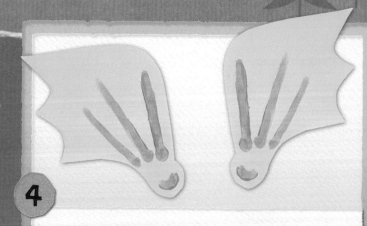

4 Cut two dragon wings out of yellow paper. Draw lines on your wings, like this, then tape them to either side of your dragon.

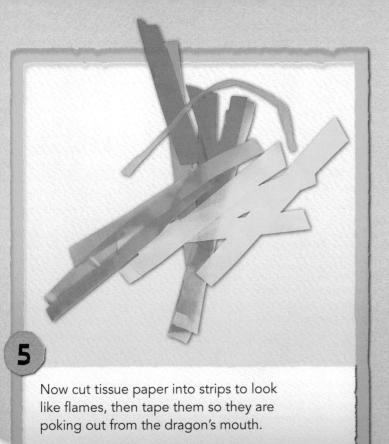

5

Now cut tissue paper into strips to look like flames, then tape them so they are poking out from the dragon's mouth.

6

For the fangs, cut two triangles from white paper or card and stick them in place.

I AM NOT AN EGGBOX...

I AM A SLIPPERY SNAKE!

Cut the egg cups out of a large eggbox and paint them your favourite snaky colours. Use a pencil to carefully make a hole in the top of each cup, then thread a piece of string through. Finish your snake with a forked tongue and googly eyes!

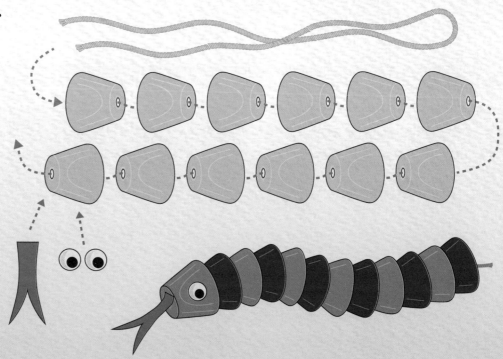

WHALE!

I LOVE **SQUIRTING** WATER FROM THE **BLOW HOLE** ON MY BACK, SO YOU'D **BETTER** GET YOUR **RAINCOAT** READY IF WE'RE GOING TO **HANG OUT.**

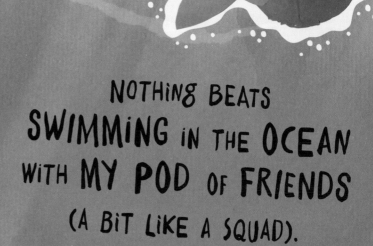

NOTHING BEATS **SWIMMING** IN THE **OCEAN** WITH **MY POD** OF **FRIENDS** (A BIT LIKE A SQUAD).

YOU WILL NEED

- ONE EGGBOX
- BLUE PAINT
- BLUE PAPER
- PENS
- PENCILS
- GLUE
- TAPE
- SAFE SCISSORS
- BLUE TISSUE PAPER
- TIN FOIL

SET THE SCENE

Make a watery scene from blue tissue paper or by painting a piece of card. You could make your own fish and other sea creatures from colourful paper or foil to stick in the sea, too! To make your wonderful water-blowing whale, turn the page.

GO FURTHER!

ON THE NEXT PAGE, WE'LL SHOW YOU HOW TO MAKE A WIBBLY WOBBLY JELLYFISH AND AN AWESOMELY COOL TURTLE. SO LET'S GO!

WHY DID THE WHALE CROSS THE ROAD?

TO GET TO THE OTHER TIDE!

DID YOU KNOW?
WHALES BREATHE AIR THROUGH THE BLOWHOLE IN THE TOP OF THEIR HEAD.

I AM NOT AN EGGBOX...
I'M A WHALE!

1

For the whale's body, carefully cut one egg cup from your eggbox. Paint this blue and leave it to one side to dry.

2

Cut two fin shapes and one tail shape from blue card or paper.

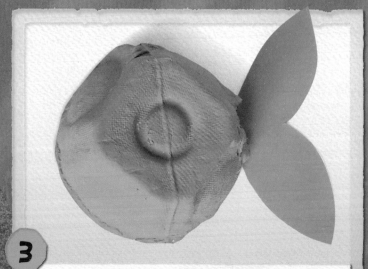

3

When the paint has dried, tape the tail to the back of your cup using some sticky tape.

4

Tear blue tissue paper and tin foil into strips to look like streams of water.

5 Use a pencil to make a hole in the top of your whale, then twist your strips of paper and foil together and push through the hole. Tape inside to hold in place.

6 Stick a fin on each side of your whale and finish off with googly eyes and a big smile.

I AM NOT AN EGGBOX...

I AM A JELLYFISH AND A TURTLE!

Use the same technique to make a jellyfish or a turtle. Tape lengths of wool underneath a painted eggcup to make your jellyfish. Add green paper legs and a pompom head to make your turtle. Finish them both with googly eyes from your book.

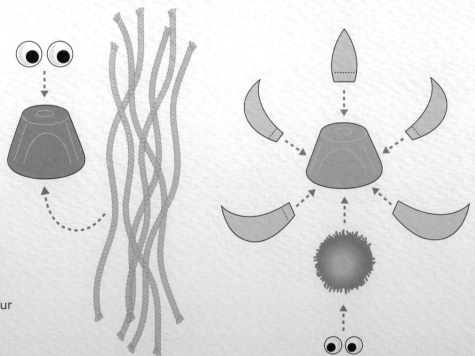

MUSIC SHAKERS!

WE'RE A BAND OF **MERRY MUSIC MAKERS.** GIVE US A **RATTLE** AND MAKE A **SWEET BEAT.**

WE ARE **PACKED** WITH **DRIED BEANS** AND WE CREATE THE **MUSIC OF DREAMS.**

SHAKE!

YOU WILL NEED

- ONE EGGBOX
- SAFETY SCISSORS
- UNCOOKED RICE
- TAPE
- PAINTS
- BRUSHES

SET THE SCENE

Make a stage suitable for a rockstar! Use a brown card base and add blue or red strips as the curtain. Sprinkle with glitter for added sparkle! Now turn over the page to make your own music band!

DID YOU KNOW? SHAKERS LIKE THESE ARE PART OF THE PERCUSSION FAMILY OF INSTRUMENTS.

RATTLE!

ROLL!

GO FURTHER!

COOL DOWN AFTER ALL THAT MUSIC MAKING WITH A CARTON OF DELICIOUS ICE CREAMS! TURN OVER THE PAGE TO FIND OUT HOW.

I AM NOT AN EGGBOX...
I'M A MUSIC SHAKER!

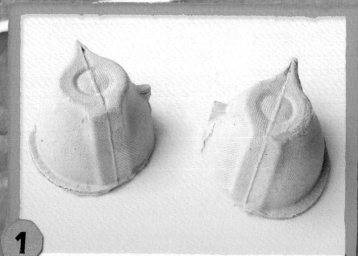

1 Carefully cut two egg cups out of your eggbox.

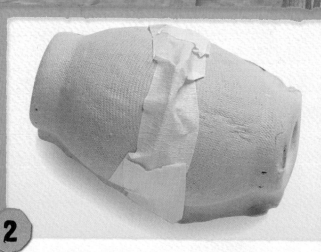

2 Fill one egg cup with uncooked rice and tape the second egg cup to the top like a lid. Make sure the tape completely seals any gaps.

3 Draw some patterns on your shaker before adding colour with your paints. We chose spots, stripes and star prints.

4 Leave your shaker to dry completely and get ready to make some music!

5

To complete your brilliant band, try switching the ingredients inside to see what different sounds you can make. Try out these ideas:

- raw lentils
- uncooked pasta
- dried beans
- rice
- corn kernels

I AM NOT AN EGGBOX...

I AM AN ICE CREAM PARLOUR!

Cut the central dividers out of the bottom of an eggbox. Flip them upside down to make your ice cream cone shape. Use pompoms for the ice cream and small beads for the sprinkles. Then use another eggbox to stand your ice creams in.

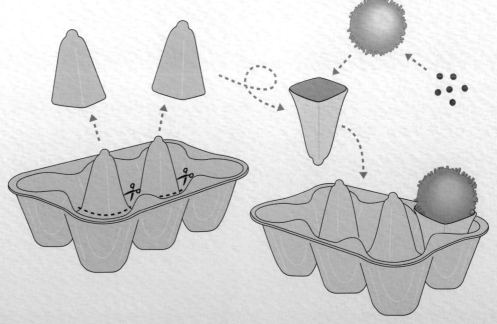

CAR!

BEEP! BEEP! BEEP! BEEP!

VROOM! I AM NOT AN EGGBOX, I AM A SUPER SPEEDY CAR.

YOU WILL NEED

- ONE EGGBOX
- SAFETY SCISSORS
- PAINTBRUSHES
- PAINT
- TINFOIL
- GLUE
- BUTTONS

WITH A **HONK** OF MY HORN AND A **ROAR** OF MY **ENGINE**, I'LL BE WITH YOU IN **NO TIME!**

SET THE SCENE

Make an exciting race track to zoom your cars around on. Just paint or draw your road design onto a large piece of paper. Add trees and tunnels to make your road more exciting. Now, turn over to make your own colourful car.

GO FURTHER!

IF TRAINS ARE YOUR THING, YOU CAN FIND OUT HOW TO MAKE ONE ON THE NEXT PAGE.

1 Cut an egg cup out of your eggbox.

2 Paint the egg cup in your favourite colour and leave it to dry, completely.

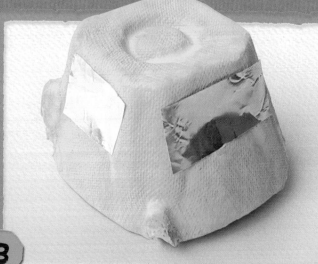

3 Once dry, cut some windows out of tin foil and glue them onto the car.

4 Scrunch up bits of tin foil into little balls to make headlights and tail-lights.

5 Find four matching buttons and glue two to either side of your car to make wheels.

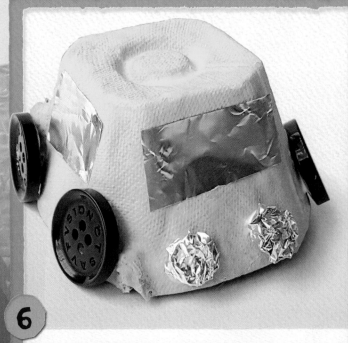

6 Glue on your headlights and tail lights to complete your car.

I AM NOT AN EGGBOX...

I AM A STEAM TRAIN!

Cut an eggbox into thirds. Paint two the same colour, and one a different colour. Attach the painted cars together using string and tape. Add two more cups to the front of the train to make a funnel as shown. Glue on some cotton wool for steam and buttons for wheels.

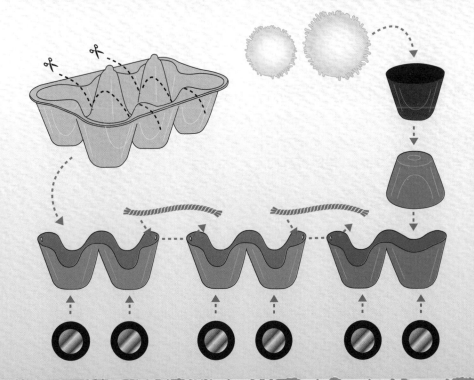

YOUR DESIGNS

NOW IT'S OVER TO YOU... THE ONLY THING HOLDING YOUR EGGBOX BACK FROM GREATNESS IS YOUR OWN IMAGINATION! SKETCH YOUR IDEAS HERE - WE'VE GIVEN YOU A COUPLE OF OUTLINES TO GET YOU STARTED.

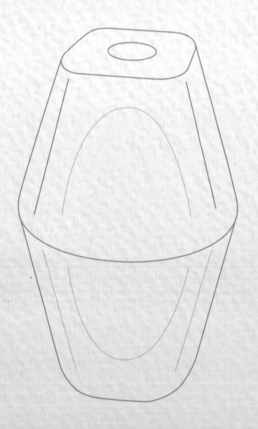 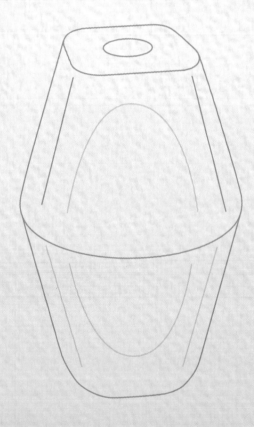

. . . .

penguin feet

penguin beaks

hen wings

pirate ship sail badges

fire engine strips

pirate ship bunting

pirate ship anchor

whale tail

dragon wings